Prickly
and
Soft
Animals

by Barbara J. Behm
Illustrated by Martin Camm,
John Francis, and Dick Twinney

Gareth Stevens Publishing
MILWAUKEE

For a free color catalog describing Gareth Stevens Publishing's list of high-quality books
and multimedia programs, call 1-800-542-2595 (USA) or 1-800-461-9120 (Canada).
Gareth Stevens Publishing's Fax: (414) 225-0377.

Library of Congress Cataloging-in-Publication Data

Behm, Barbara J., 1952-
    Prickly and soft animals / by Barbara J. Behm; illustrated by Martin Camm, John Francis,
and Dick Twinney.
       p. cm. — (Animal opposites)
    Includes index.
    Summary: Introduces ten animals that can be distinguished by how they feel to the touch,
including the porcupine, galago, spiny anteater, chinchilla, stickleback, llama, hedgehog,
giant panda, tenrec, and rabbit.
    ISBN 0-8368-2460-1 (lib. bdg.)
    1. Animals—Miscellanea—Juvenile literature. [1. Animals.] I. Camm, Martin, ill.
II. Francis, John, 1942- ill. III. Twinney, Dick, ill. IV. Title. V. Series: Animal
opposites (Milwaukee, Wis.)
QL49.B536   1999
590—dc21   99-33300

This North American edition first published in 1999 by
Gareth Stevens Publishing
1555 North RiverCenter Drive, Suite 201
Milwaukee, WI 53212 USA

This edition © 1999 by Gareth Stevens, Inc. Created with original © 1997 by Horus Editions
Limited, a division of Award Publications Limited, 1st Floor, 27 Longford Street, London NW1 3DZ,
U.K. Additional end matter © 1999 by Gareth Stevens, Inc.

Cover illustrations: a porcupine and a llama

Printed in the United States of America

1 2 3 4 5 6 7 8 9 03 02 01 00 99

Contents

Porcupine

The porcupine is a prickly animal.

The porcupine scares its enemies with needle-sharp quills. The other animals run!

Porcupines eat leaves,
bark, buds, and twigs.

Galago

*The galago is a
soft animal.*

The galago has a long,
bushy tail, just like a
squirrel's. Its fur is
thick and woolly.

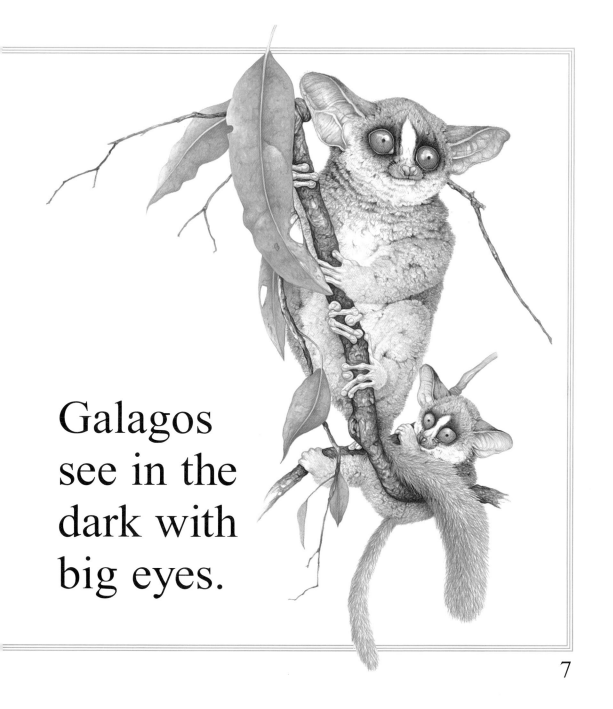

Galagos
see in the
dark with
big eyes.

Spiny Anteater

The spiny anteater is a prickly animal.

The spiny anteater is covered with spines. Its hair feels rough to the touch.

Spiny anteaters lick up
ants with their tongues.

Chinchilla

*The chinchilla is a
soft animal.*

The chinchilla lives
high in the mountains
of South America. It
has a soft, warm coat.

Chinchillas eat
seeds, fruit, and herbs.

Stickleback

The stickleback is a prickly animal.

The stickleback is small with beautiful colors. It has bony spines along its body.

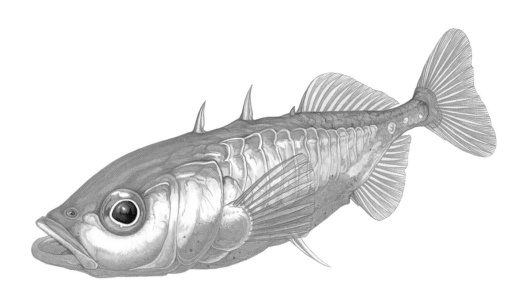

Spines keep sticklebacks
safe from predators.

Llama

*The llama is a
soft animal.*

The llama looks like
a woolly camel with no
hump. It lives high in
the mountains.

Llamas can walk for hours without getting tired.

Hedgehog

The hedgehog is a prickly animal.

The hedgehog has about five thousand very sharp spines all over its back and face.

Hedgehogs curl into
balls when in danger.

Giant Panda

The giant panda is a soft animal.

The giant panda has a thick, black-and-white coat. It is one of the world's rarest animals.

Giant pandas live in the
mountains of China.

Tenrec

The tenrec is a prickly animal.

The tenrec has orange, black, and white spines. It lives on the island of Madagascar.

20

Tenrecs hunt for food
with their snouts.

Rabbit

*The rabbit is a
soft animal.*

The rabbit has soft, silky fur and a fluffy tail. It even has soft, fluffy feet.

Rabbits
have
excellent
hearing.

Glossary

enemies: living things that are harmful or deadly.

herbs: plants used for medicine and flavoring.

predators: animals that hunt other animals.

quills: sharp spines on some animals' bodies.

rare: very few in number.

spines: pointed, bony objects found on certain animals' bodies.

Index